LOOKS

G·R·E·A·T!

Exciting Ways of Presenting Your Projects

David Deakin
Gordon Moore

Pembroke Publishers Limited

Published in Canada in 1992 by
Pembroke Publishers Limited,
538 Hood Road
Markham, Ontario, L3R 3K9
(416) 477-0650 Fax (416) 477-3691

© David Deakin & Gordon Moore 1989

First published 1990 by Dellasta Pty Ltd

Canadian Cataloguing in Publication Data

Deakin, David
  Looks great! : exciting ways of presenting
your projects

ISBN 0-921217-82-X

1. Graphic arts – Juvenile literature. 2. Book
design – Juvenile literature. 1. Moore, Gordon.
II. Title.

NC655.D32 1992   j741.6   C92-094687-9

The activities in this book are intended for children working under
supervision. While every effort has been made to ensure that the
activities are safe, neither the publisher nor the authors can be held
liable for loss or damage to persons or property caused by or resulting
from the carrying out of any activity described herein.

We wish to thank the following people:

NASA for permission to reproduce the photograph of the astronaut on
pages 24 and 25.

Thank you Deborah, Jessica and Alexander for all the time that this
book stole from you. And my fellow centurion time bandit, thank you
for the inspiration (and the biscuits).

Gordon

Text by Mike Smith
Designed by David Deakin and Gordon Moore
Printed and bound in Canada by Webcom Limited
098765432

Contents

Introduction

So you've been given a project to do. Okay! And you've looked in all the books you can find, and read all the things you can, and you've written it all out in rough.

But whether it's a single page project or a long publishing assignment, we all know that writing the thing is only the first stage. Now you've got to decide on how you're going to *present* it. And unless you want to present it as a boring dry old piece of writing that will put everyone (including yourself) to sleep, you're going to need some inspiration . . .

. . . and that's where this book is going to come into its own!

Read through this book. By the end you'll have so many ideas on how to present your project that your teacher will just have to say that it *looks great!* and give you top marks . . .

So — here we go!

Where do I start?

It's all too hard.

But I can't draw!

Everything I do looks messy and my teacher never likes it anyway. I never know what to do and I never know where to start.

It won't be any good!

Mine always look boring and silly. I never know how to make projects look exciting. They always look the worst. I hate projects.

I'm extinct...

... but I come alive whenever projects on dinosaurs are beautifully presented. Assignments aren't difficult to put together if you know how, and this book will show you that making them exciting is as easy as falling off a skateboard.

W hat a mess! This certainly doesn't *Look Great*, does it?

Start with a nice clean sheet – not last Friday's lunch wrapper!

Wash your hands before you start . . .

Crumbs . . . this really takes the cake for a currant project!

Masking tape is very useful for masking things – and good for sticking torn pictures together, but only if used on the *back* of the picture.

It's probably a good idea if your teacher *doesn't* feel seasick after reading your text: use light pencil lines that you can rub out later.

A great idea to use a coloured background, but what a messy way to do it!

Captions are a great idea, but only if they explain what the picture is!

The picture would look great if you'd cut it out more carefully.

A nice heading if only we could read it!

Is this a border . . . or is it a track made by a blind caterpillar dipped in soy sauce???

. . . Don't eat or drink while you're working!

Don't scrub words out. Write carefully and clearly. If you do make mistakes, white them out.

Very nice – but what is it??

Don't sign your name unless you're really proud of your work

It's easier than you think.

The last page was really yuk!

Let's take the same bits and pieces and make a one-page poster that really *Looks Great!*

Before You Begin

1 Clean off your desk.
2 Wash your hands.
3 Get a piece of cardboard ready as a cutting board.

Rough out your project first. Work out where you want things to be positioned. That way you won't make mistakes on your good copy.

Draw a light pencil line down the exact centre of the sheet. This helps you get the title in the centre, and will help with the positioning of the pictures and the writing too.

Remember – this is only one way of laying out a one-page project: in this book you'll discover many more.

...and on the right, that's my Uncle Arthur

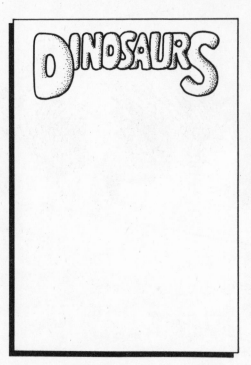

The best place to start is with a good clear heading that is fun to look at.

Pictures can be made more interesting if you paste them onto coloured shapes.

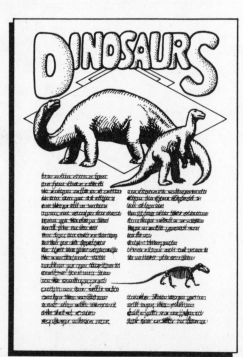

Lightly pencil in the lines where you'll be writing. It can be made easier to read if you break it up with small pictures, and make two or more columns.

Add a fancy border. Rub out the pencil lines – and there you are. *Looks Great!*

DINOSAURS

Laying it out.

There are lots of ways you can lay out a project and this section shows you some of the things you can do.

Layout is important not only for one-sheet projects but also for longer assignments – particularly the first page. After all, it's first impressions that count!

(By the way, the actual written bits are shown on these layouts by the use of straight lines like this.) →

Allow plenty of space for your headings, and don't make your writing too small. Remember, it is very important that your project is easy to read.

A project on maple trees needs a good border. You'll find lots of ideas for stylish borders on pages 39-43.

This is one simple way of doing a layout. The big letter 'M' is the first letter of the first word of your text.

You can make your layout a bit different by changing around the heading, the pictures and the text . . .

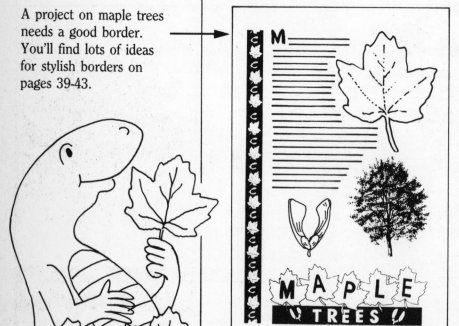

. . . Or you can enlarge one of the pictures using a photocopier.

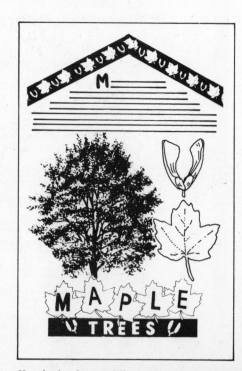

Use the borders in different sizes, and centre all the text. See what a difference it's made.

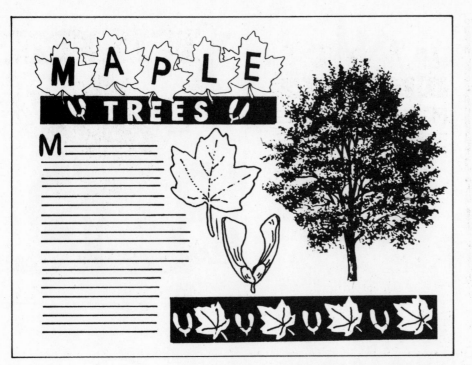

On this page are some examples of what you can do if you choose different shapes and sizes for your one-page assignments.

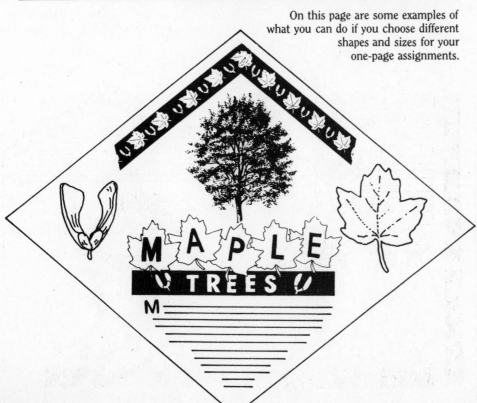

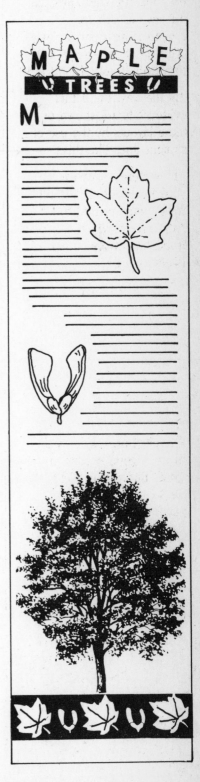

Lively letters.

reating fancy letters can be great fun, especially if you can make them suit the theme they are describing. The letters on the next few pages all do this: See if you can guess what the theme is for each of the first five letters.

You can make a complete alphabet of letters, and use them to create whole headings, or you can just design one and use that as the first letter of the very first word of your text. To see how this is done, look at the letter 'C' at the top of this page.

. . Or you can just use a stencil and a bit of imagination to create letters like the ones on this first page!

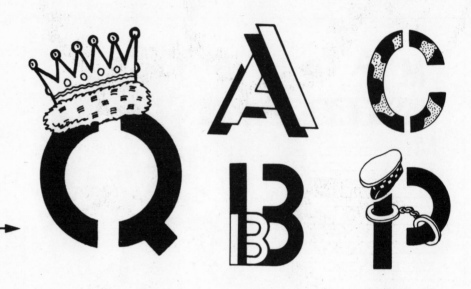

Wool

Night

Messy

Brush

Children

Iron

Glutton

Paper

Spooky

Tree

Road

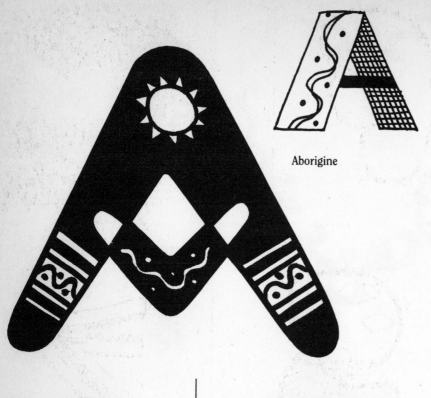

Aborigine

Rock

Happy

Fishing

Finger

Shaky

String

Water

Fairy

Wood

Rainforest

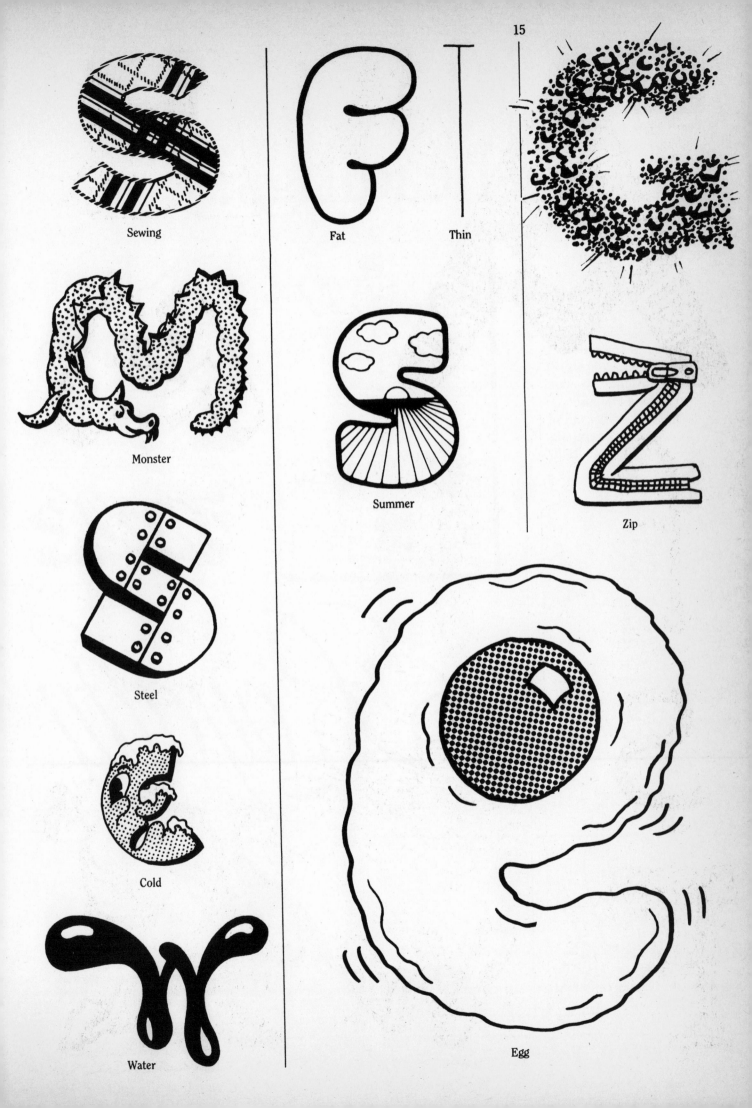

Sewing

Fat

Thin

Monster

Summer

Zip

Steel

Cold

Water

Egg

Here are lots of ideas on how to create great headings. You might recognise some of the letters from the previous pages!

Headings can be as mad as you like – as long as they are readable! The more unusual they are, the more interested everyone will be in reading what you've written!

Remember, if you can't think of an inspiring way of drawing the letters, you can try something else: use a stencil, cut the titles out of fabric, or paper, or even cut them out of the page itself!

How about headings?

GOLD

WATER

FOD

E

Here are lots more headings that describe the subject of the project.

Remember: the trick is to think of something that's typical for your subject and use it in the heading. For convicts, you can use chains; for rainforests, vines; for a zoo, you can use animals.

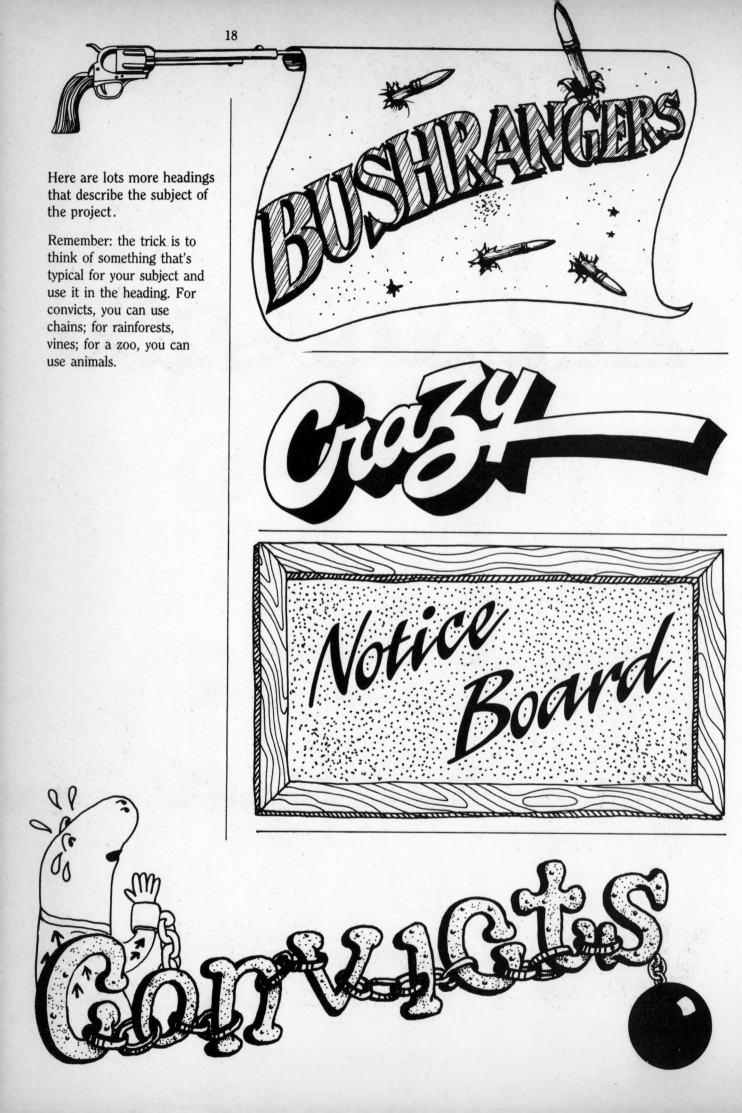

RAIN-FOREST

TENSE?

FLOWERS

VICTORIANA

It's not too difficult to create stylish headings. You can use almost anything: your own monsters, animals or cartoon characters, or even something like the 'fingers' title, which was drawn by a high school student.

. . . and putting a heading onto a drawing can be delicious!

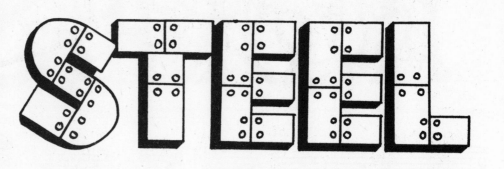

ROCK and Roll

Publishing

FINGERS

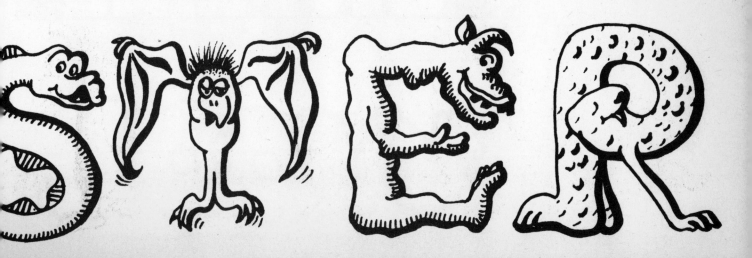

SPIDER

.... And here are still more ideas for headings, all of them winners.

It really isn't hard to make up great headings. Anyone can do it. It just takes a little thought.

Best of luck!

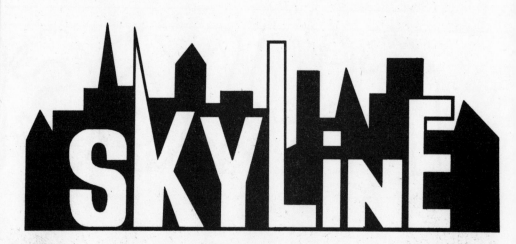

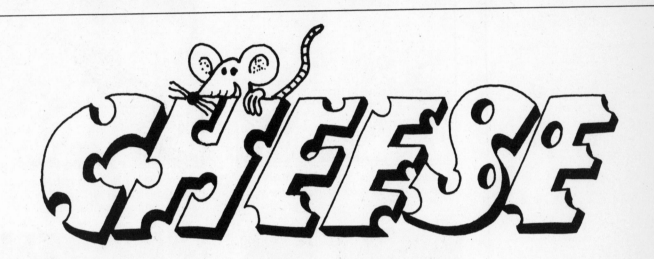

SPACE

CHEESE

CATS

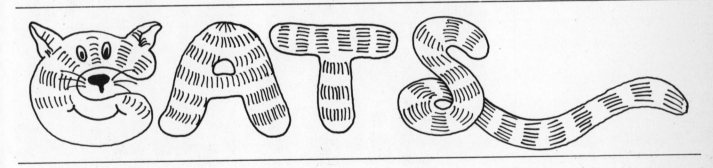

Pollution

his is where the fun starts!

The next eight pages will show you some great ways for using pictures in your projects. Cutting them out, photocopying them or tracing them are three simple ways to get you started.

The easiest way you can make pictures more interesting is by cutting them into different sizes and shapes.

Don't just use the photocopier to get identical copies of your original: use it to create stunning effects!

Most kids do tracings by drawing round the outlines of a picture. But there are other ways of making tracings. The simplest is to use different sorts of lines and make your copy look like an original drawing!

Read on . . . there's lots more to follow!

Playing with pictures.

The simplest method is to cut out the complete drawing and stick it onto the page.

You can make it more interesting by cutting round the figures in the top part and only using straight cuts for the bottom.

Here's a great picture of a man walking on the moon.

You can make the picture more dramatic by enlarging it and cutting parts of it off.

Here's a photo of Dave's cat. It's OK, but . . . well . . . not exactly exciting.

Doing a tracing of it makes it a bit more interesting, especially if you fill in the shadows with solid black.

You can concentrate attention on one feature by cutting a starburst round it.

You can cut out one small part of the picture and enlarge it.

Or you can cut out just one part of the illustration and colour some of it.

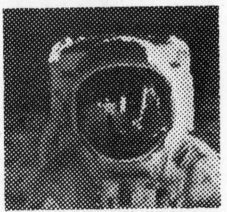

You can concentrate on one part of the picture, and enlarge it to show the dots that make up the printed image.

You can do something really unusual by putting together multiple images.

Or, for a really special effect, try creating an exploded picture by cutting the photo in lots of pieces.

Try filling the shadows with lots of long lines close together going in different directions.

You can do your tracing by using dots for the shadows. The closer the dots, the darker the shadow will look.

Here's another effect you can try. Use short heavy lines for the shadows.

Cut it out.

On these two pages we've gone completely *wacky,* just to give you an idea of what you can do with a pair of scissors and something to cut.

You can have a lot of fun making up your own pictures using coloured paper and pictures from magazines or newspapers.

Of course you *can* use whole pictures, but you can also cut them into different shapes like the body of a snake or the trunk of an elephant.

If you're feeling really ambitious, you should try making complete scenes out of photographs and coloured paper.

The rubbish bin and the palm tree were cut out of coloured paper and combined with photographs from magazines to create a stunning effect.

You are only limited by your imagination with this technique!

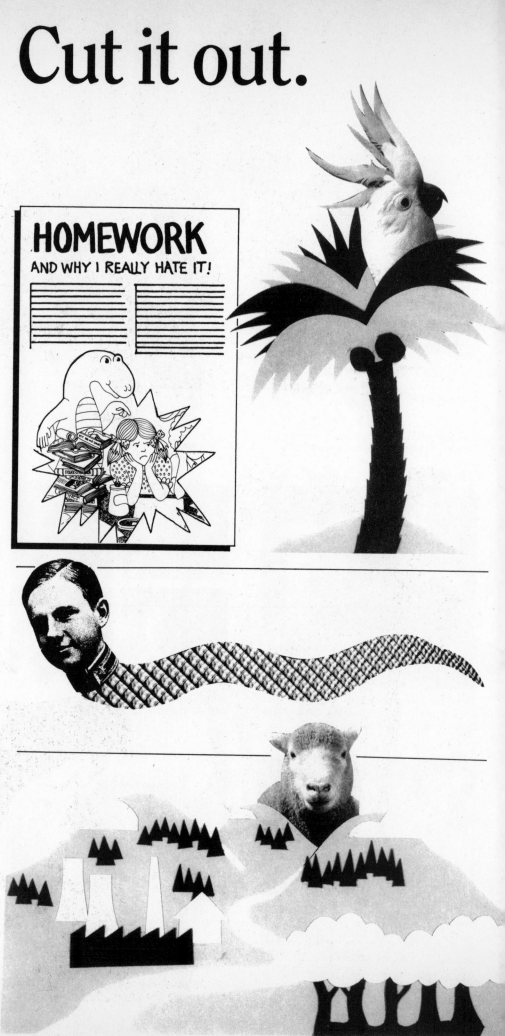

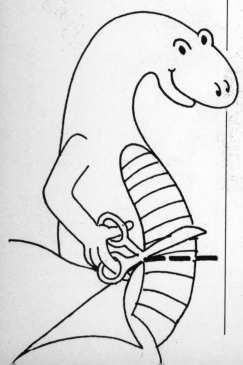

Make a friend of a photocopier.

If your school will let you use a photocopier (or if you can get copies made at a store), you can really do some fancy stuff with photocopiers.

If you can get to use a photocopier that enlarges and reduces, you're in luck. If your illustration's really small, just keep on enlarging it again and again until it's the right size – or if the original's too big, keep reducing it until it's the size you want.

You can put colour into your project by photocopying onto green or red or blue paper – or if you're rich (or lucky) you can get a full colour copy of your original.

Here is a simple but effective layout using an enlarged photocopy.

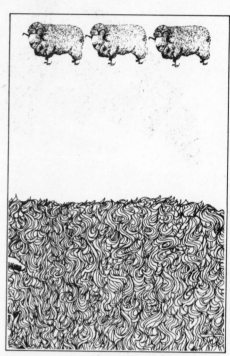

You can create special effects by really blowing up one small part of a picture. The bottom half of this page is part of one of the sheep at the top!

Or you can try taking a few photocopies of the same thing and sticking them one on top of the other.

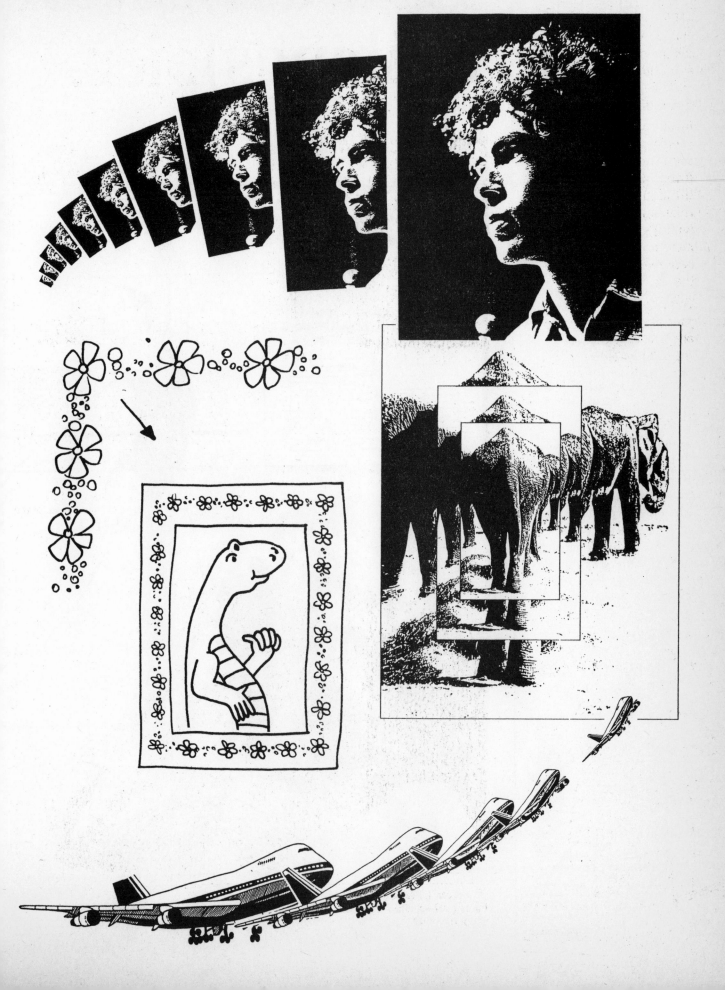

Try tracings (or rubbings).

You've done loads of tracings in the past. But from now on your tracing's going to be very different — it's going to be fun and it's going to be dramatic.

Basic tracing is very easy. All you need is thin paper, a pen or a pencil. If the paper you're using is too thick to see through, try putting the picture you're tracing up against a bright light, like a window.

Experiment with thick lines, thin lines and solid blocks of colour, and before long you'll be making tracings that look like original drawings, or better.

Here are lots of great ideas for different tracing styles.

Another way is to cut around a shape and project it onto a sheet of paper using an overhead projector. This is a great way to get the outline of a really big image. You can fill in the detail or decorate the inside however you like. Have a look at *Try Something Tricky* for some ideas.

RUBBINGS

The drawings below here were made by gently rubbing a soft pencil over a piece of paper on top of an object, or a textured surface.

Try rubbing a wooden surface to create an interesting background to a title . . . or be a bit more creative and do the rubbing in the shape of a tree.

At last! We've covered the basics, so now we're at the stage of getting it all together. Over the next few pages is a range of finished projects that have been put together using ideas and techniques covered in this book.

Getting it all together.

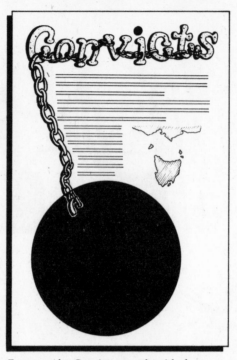

For example, *Convicts* uses the title from an earlier section of the book.

The illustration of the musicians is a tracing that has been filled in solid.

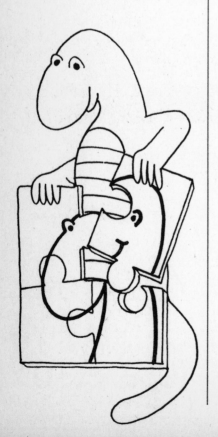

Recognise the 'T' in the title?

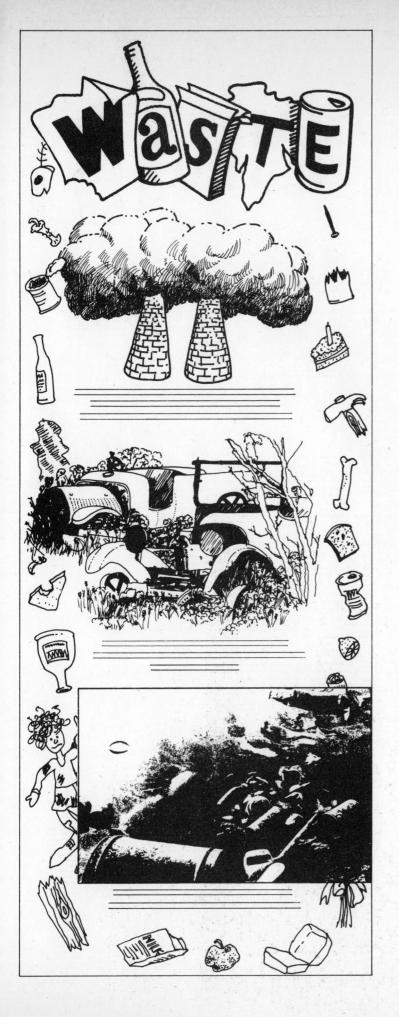

PHARAOHS

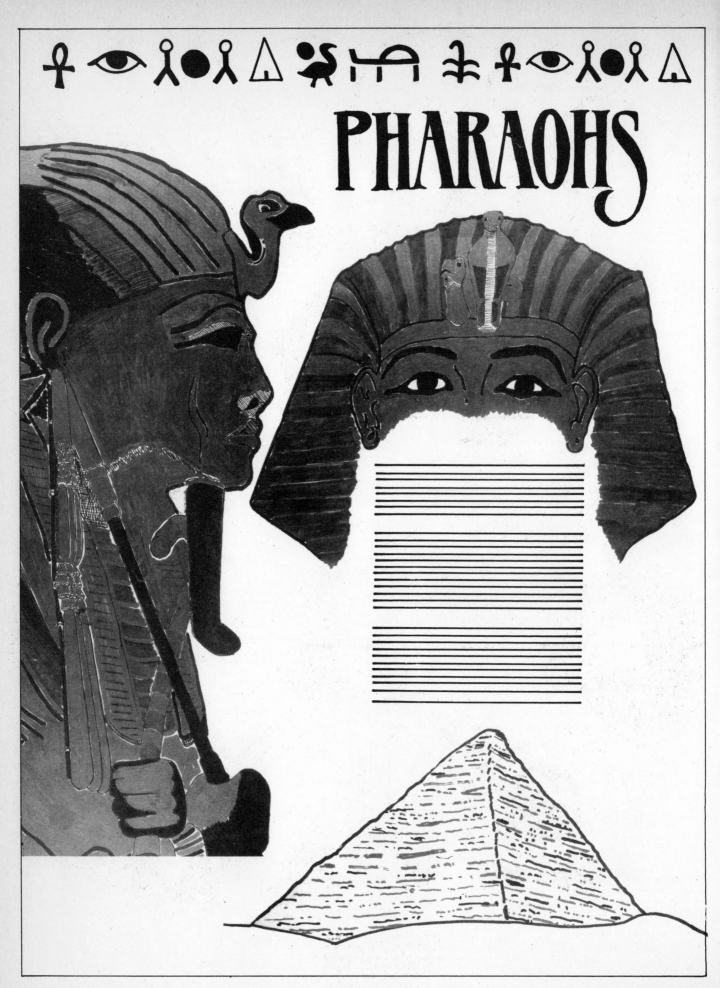

The drawings in this project are by
Christopher Andrews, aged 13.

PEOPLE
IN MY WORLD

veryone can draw!

All you need is a little confidence, a piece of paper and a pencil.

The trick is to keep the drawings simple — And have fun! You don't need to draw like a professional to make people look twice at your work. Don't even try to make your drawings as good as photographs. Instead, try for a simple outline using simple shapes.

Simple lines and shapes are all that we needed for this project called *On the Beach*, and to create our little mate the dinosaur.

Circles, clouds, buckets can all be used as the starting point for lots of different drawings.

Even people are easy if you start with simple stick shapes!

Everyone's an artist.

Want to practise a bit first? Try a few monsters. They might not be any good for your project, but they'll look great on the covers of your notebooks!

Put on a border.

B·b·B·b·B·b·B
b   B
B   b B
B   b B
b·B·b·B·b·B orders, borders, borders. What's a border you might ask?

A border can be used to frame your complete work, to highlight a special part of it, or just to underline your heading.

You can draw neat borders with a ruler, but you can make great ones without a ruler, too. They can be as simple as a dotted line or as complicated as a tangle of snakes. Remember, borders don't have to be all-round ones, either: you can make classy ones by creating interesting corners and then linking them with a simple line or two.

It's a good idea to choose a border that reflects the theme of the assignment.

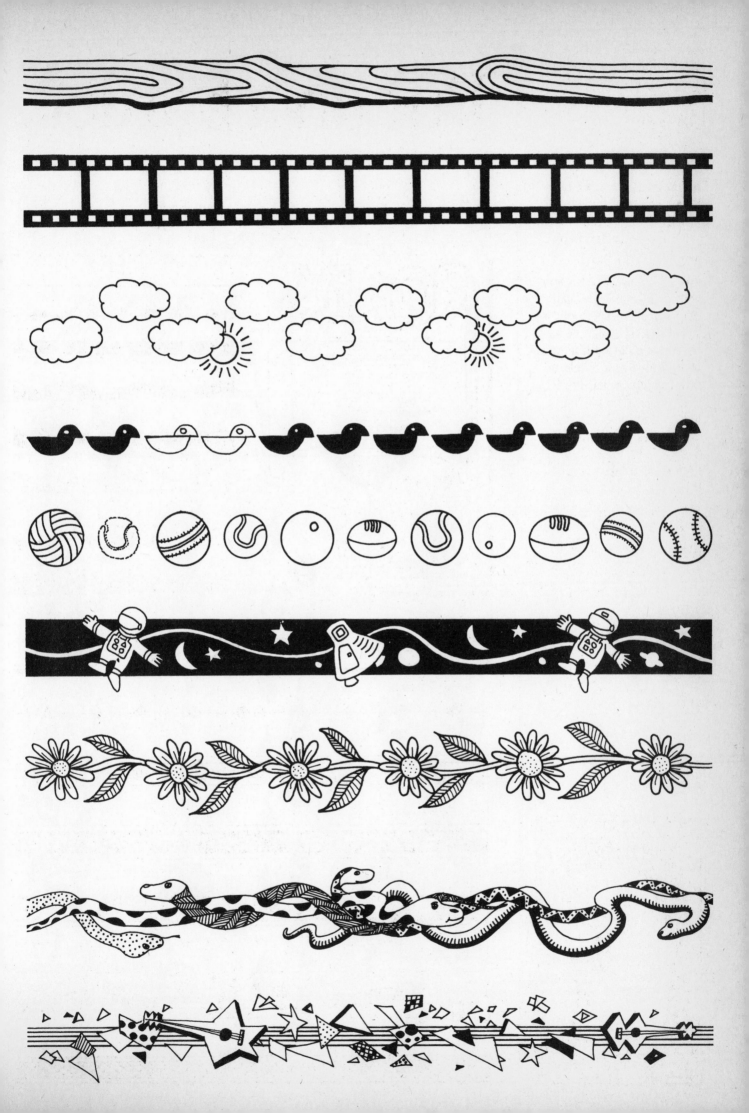

40

Here are lots more borders to inspire you. And if they don't grab you, you might find what you're looking for in the next four pages. But don't forget to keep your eyes open when you read other books or magazines. They have lots of ideas, too!

stand by to repel borders

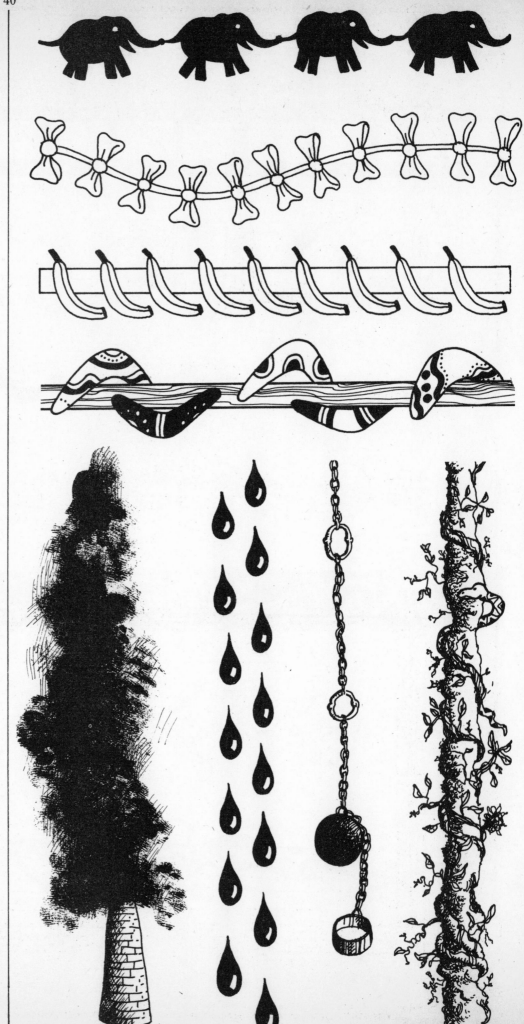

Here are some corners just waiting for lines
to connect them up.

Alphabet soup.

Here are some sets of letters that can be used in projects and assignments.

There's a big difference between using letters and using your own drawings. You have to align each letter very carefully or the whole thing looks quite messy.

If you do decide to use letters like this, draw a light pencil line on your page and make sure that the bottom of each letter *just* touches your line.

You can use any of these alphabets as a starting point to create your own letters like these.

ABCDEFG
HIJKLMN
OPQRSTU
VWXYZ
1234567
890

ABCDEFG
HIJKLMN
OPQRST
UVWXYZ
abcdefghi
jklmnopqr
stuvwxyz
123456789

ABCDEFGHIJ
KLMNOPQRS
TUVWXYZ
abcdefghijklmn
opqrstuvwxyz
1234567890

ABCDEFGHIJKLMN
OPQRSTUVWXYZ*ab*
cdefghijklmnopqrst
uvwxyz 1234567890

ABCDEFGHIJKLM
NOPQRSTUVWX
YZ 1234567890

ABCDEFGHIJK
LMNOPQRST
UVWXYZ
1234567890

ABCDEFGHIJKLMNOPQRS
TUVWXYZ abcdefghijklmnopqr
stuvwxyz 1234567890

ABCDEFGHIJKLMNO
PQRSTUVWXYZ abcdef
ghijklmnopqrstuvwxyz
1234567890

ABCDEFGHIJKLMN
OPQRSTUVWXYZ
1234567890

ABCDEFGHIJKLMN
OPQRSTUVWXYZ
abcdefghijklmnopqrstu
vwxyz 1234567890

ABCDEFGHIJKLMN
OPQRSTUVWXYZ
1234567890

ABCDEFGHIJKLMNOP
QRSTUVWXYZ
abcdefghijklmnopqrst
uvwxyz
1234567890

ABCDEFGHIJKLMN
OPQRSTUVWXYZ
1234567890

ABCDEFGHIJKLMNO
PQRSTUVWXYZ abc
defghijklmnopqrst
uvwxyz1234567890

ABCDEFGHIJKL
MNOPQRSTUVW
XYZ1234567890

ABCDEFGHIJKL
MNOPQRSTUVW
XYZ 1234567890

ABCDEFGHIJKL
MNOPQRSTUVW
XYZ 1234567890

ABCDEFGHIJKLM
NOPQRSTUVWX
YZ 1234567890

ABCDEFGHIJKLMNOPQR
STUVWXYZ
abcdefghijklmnopqrstuv
wxyz 1234567890

Up to now we've been looking mainly at single pages: but often assignments are too long to be on one page. So here are a few ideas on how to present an assignment in book form.

In books there is one basic rule: all the pages should follow a similar basic layout. That doesn't mean that they all have to look the same, though! If you want two columns of text, then each page must have two columns, but where you put the pictures and how big they are is up to you. All the examples in this section follow that one basic rule.

Worm your way into books.

A book is made up of a collection of papers placed inside a cover. This book you are reading has a cover, a title page, a contents page and an introduction page before the main part of the book.

Burp!

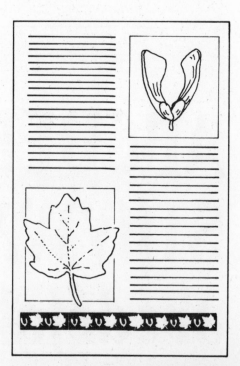

In a book it's important that all the pages follow a similar layout. In this example the text and illustrations have been broken up into two columns on each page. The pages are different but follow the same pattern.

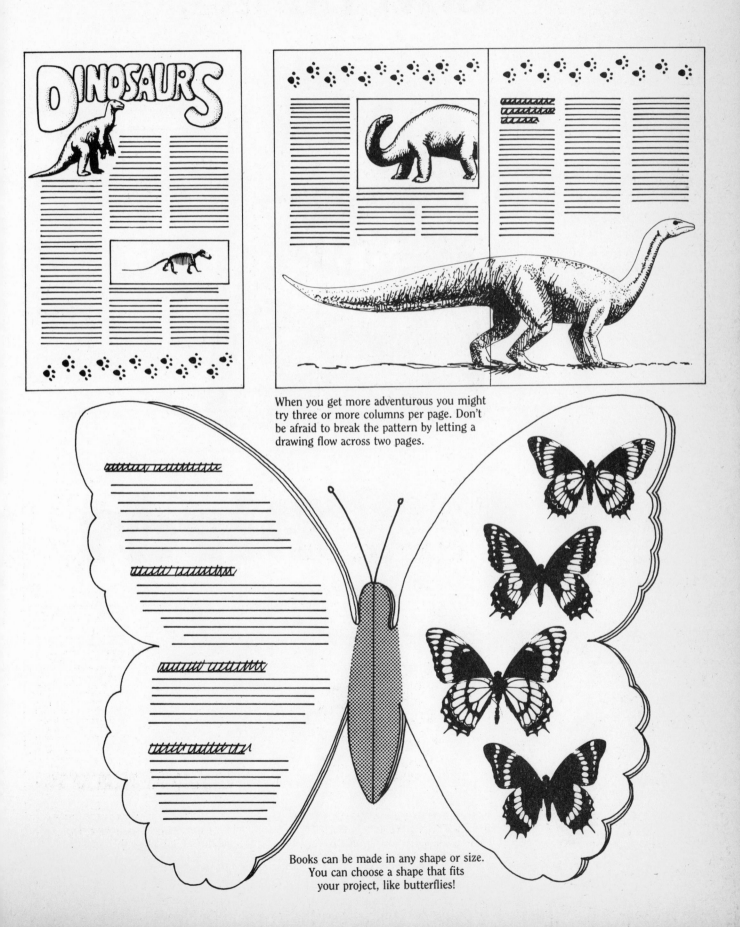

When you get more adventurous you might try three or more columns per page. Don't be afraid to break the pattern by letting a drawing flow across two pages.

Books can be made in any shape or size. You can choose a shape that fits your project, like butterflies!

I f you want people to read your assignment, you've got to give it an exciting cover. We've shown you some great covers already, but that's not all you can do.

Here are a few way-out ideas for the covers of your assignments.

Let's cover covers.

Bind the book along the top edge.

Cut slot into cover.
Stick the eyes onto the first page after the cover.

Smart lettering from 'Alphabet Soup'.

Bullet hole
(don't use a real gun, though)!

Torn edge makes the cover look more realistic.

Covers don't need to be flat! The feathers of this bird were cut out of paper, folded and stuck together to create a three dimensional cover.

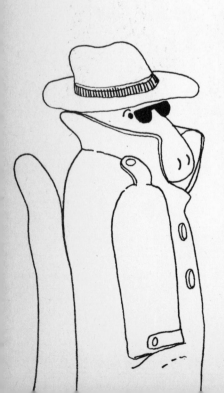

How about this for a yummy cover?

The recipe for this one is to take lots of different noodles (*before* they get to your younger brother's plate, though). Then paste them down onto a colourful background, add a tasty heading and serve it up as the cover for your next assignment on food . . .

sea

Cut the fish shapes out of the coloured plastic and put them in the plastic bag.

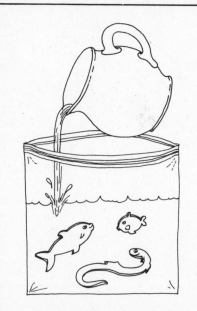

Fill the plastic bag with a small amount of water and then squeeze most of the air out of the bag before sealing it.

Want to make a real splash with your project? Try using real water!

In this swell assignment on the sea, we used some coloured plastic, a small resealable plastic bag, sandpaper, shells, coloured cardboard – and of course a little water!

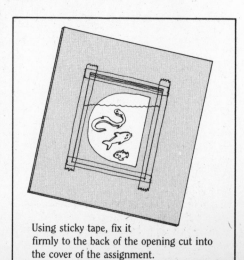

Using sticky tape, fix it firmly to the back of the opening cut into the cover of the assignment.

How about this one? All you need is a bit of telephone cord, a few cut-out stars, a tennis ball cut in half and painted, a 'spacey' heading and some hand lettering. Stick it all together and you've got a cover that's out of this world.

. . . And don't forget the astronaut bookmark!

Fun formats.

*H*ere are a few possibilities that really jump out of the page at you! They're only suggestions, but they should help you to see that you don't need to rely on drawings and photographs to make great projects.

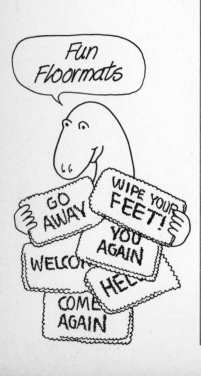

Fun Floormats

GO AWAY
WIPE YOUR FEET!
YOU AGAIN
WELCOME
HELLO
COME AGAIN

How about this for a snappy project! We used two empty cereal packets, two tops from aerosol tins and some coloured paper to make this one. The body of the assignment is in the body!

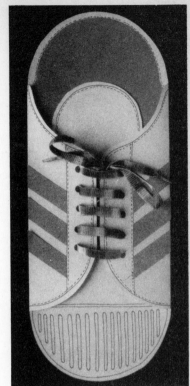

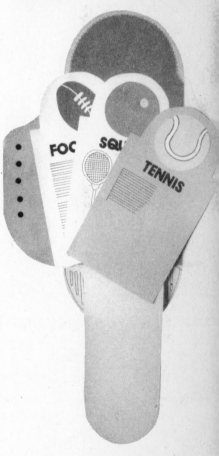

We've really put our best foot forward with this project on sport!

For this one you'll need a couple of bits of paper and a fairly long shoelace. The first piece of paper is folded so that the outside edges meet in the middle. Then it's cut into the shape of a shoe. The second piece is cut into the shape of a tongue and glued to the centre at the bottom.

Punch some lace holes, thread the lace through, and there you are.

The project cards simply slip into the inside of the laced up sports shoe, under the tongue. You can bet that no one will be able to resist undoing the laces to sneak a look at what you've written!

We've had loads of ideas for *fun formats* while we've been doing this book, but there just isn't room to put them all in. Here are a few more ideas to help you fire up your imagination.

Remember the golden rule: if you want your teacher to be really impressed by your assignment, make sure it reads well and *looks great!*

Newspapers

If you've got lots of information to present, why not write it in a newspaper! Your newspaper can be as simple or as complicated as you want to make it. If it's a really modern and up-to-date theme, try creating your newspaper on your trusty computer: it's not as hard as it sounds. If you're writing up a story from the past get a few old pictures and try to create an old fashioned paper.

Photo albums

An instant book! Put your photos into an album, and then add your text that has been written on cards.

Puzzle

Now here's a very juicy idea. Cut out some fruit shapes either from your own drawings or from photographs and stick them onto a 'tree'. You can use sticky tape and make a flap so the fruit can be lifted up, or picked right off the tree. Then you can write your project information either on the fruit itself or on the blank space underneath the fruit. A piece of (fruit) cake!

Scroll

What's more authentic for a historical project than a historical scroll! Egyptians used scrolls, and so did people in the Bible, and so probably did St George (but possibly not the Dragon).

You can make the scroll more interesting by adding papier-mâché heads, feet and tails. If you add lots of fancy lettering and decorations to the scroll itself, everyone will roll up to roll it out!

3D

Add a new dimension to your project! If you're writing a project on animals or on farming, why not build a farm scene and on the back of each animal write your project information.

You can build a 3-D project on any subject — from birds to bats, mountains to mumps!

News

If your project is on famous people or world events, a news report might be a good way to present it. Choose students to be newsreaders and reporters, draw maps, diagrams and illustrations. Your teacher might be able to video the whole thing and play it back as a television news program.

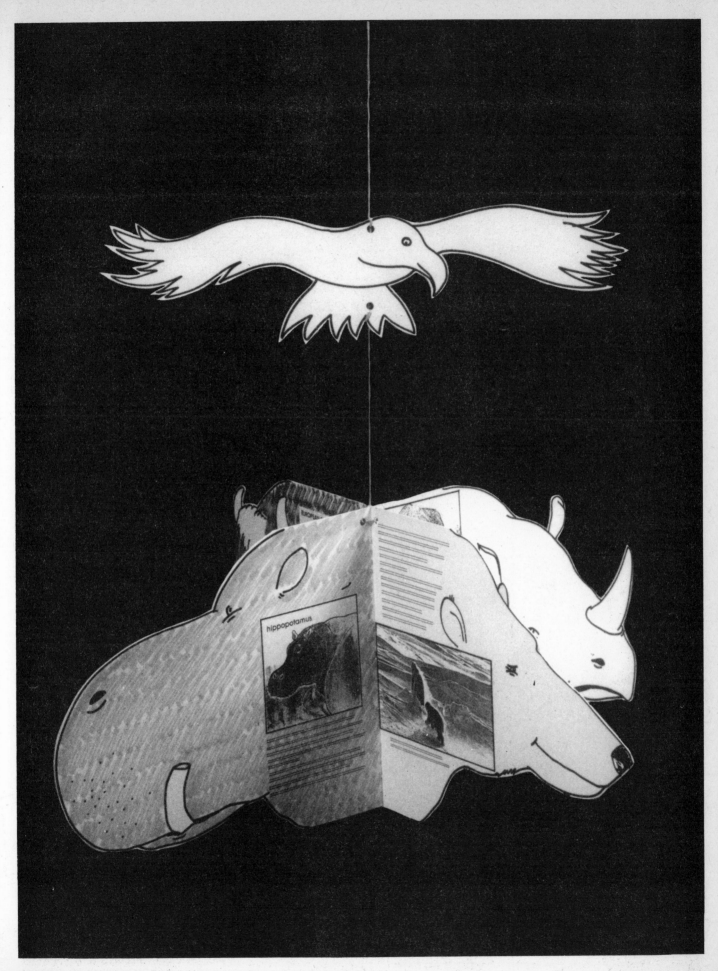

And how about a mobile? Here's a really simple idea.
Don't forget you will have to use both sides of the two pieces of cardboard!

Find two pieces of cardboard big enough for you to cut out an animal head at each end, while leaving you room to write two lots of text in the middle.

Measure exactly half way along the first piece of cardboard, and cut a slot from the top half way down. Then measure half way along the second piece, and cut a slot from

the bottom half way up. Use clear tape to hold the two pieces in place.
Attach a string from the centre and hang your mobile from the ceiling.

Ever tried potato printing? And what about candle printing? In this last section of the book, we thought you might like to try something a bit different.

Try something tricky.

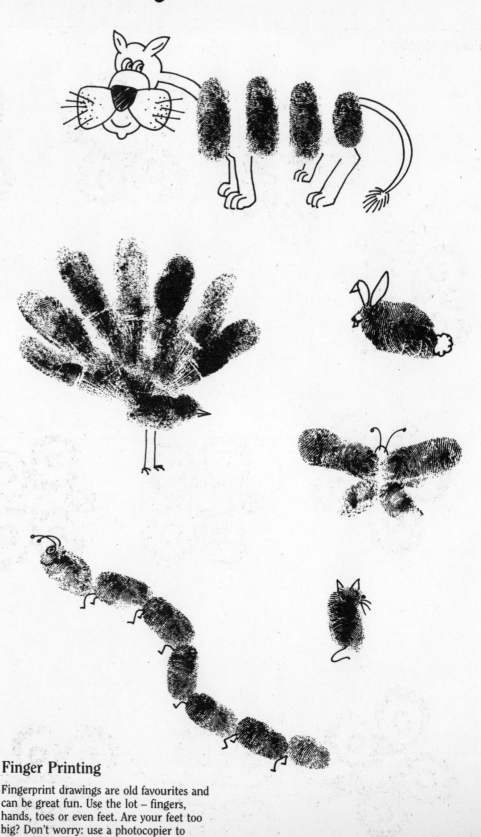

Finger Printing

Fingerprint drawings are old favourites and can be great fun. Use the lot – fingers, hands, toes or even feet. Are your feet too big? Don't worry: use a photocopier to reduce the size.

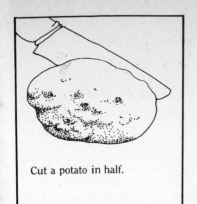
Cut a potato in half.

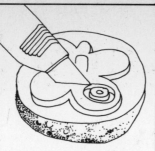
Draw your design on the cut surface, then carefully cut out the design: remember, only the raised areas will print.

Mix the colours quite thickly and paint over your design. You can use more than one colour at the same time.

For a clear print, put newspaper under the paper you're printing onto.

Potato Printing

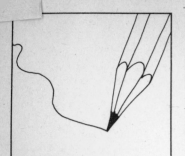 First, faintly pencil your design on the paper.

 Shave a candle so that it has a sharp edge, then draw along the pencil line with the candle, pressing hard.

 Mix a lot of thin paint.

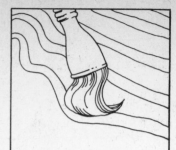 With the brush, cover the page with paint. As you do, your picture will appear.

Candle Painting